VALUED
Sales Training

VALUED
SALES TRAINING

Vol. 1

Tony Russell

Copyright © 2016 by Tony Russell.

ISBN:	Softcover	978-1-5144-9576-6
	eBook	978-1-5144-9575-9

All rights reserved. No part of this book may be reproduced or transmitted in any form or by any means, electronic or mechanical, including photocopying, recording, or by any information storage and retrieval system, without permission in writing from the copyright owner.

Any people depicted in stock imagery provided by Thinkstock are models, and such images are being used for illustrative purposes only. Certain stock imagery © Thinkstock.

Front Cover Image - zsooofija © 123RF.com
Interior Graphics
Graph Icon - donets © 123RF.com
Golf Ball - margo © 123RF.com

Print information available on the last page.

Rev. date: 06/09/2016

To order additional copies of this book, contact:
Xlibris
1-800-455-039
www.Xlibris.com.au
Orders@Xlibris.com.au

741682

Contents

Acknowledgements ix
Preface xi

1. Knowing Sales – We All Know the Story Somehow? 1
2. Prenumtive Attitude 7
3. Rocks in the Road 11
4. Pitch Tones Punctuation and Grammar 17
5. Developing Technique – Learning Curbs 21
6. Rapport 25
7. Attitude 29
8. Getting Picky 33
9. The Grove 37
10. Your Technique – With Industry Knowledge 41
11. Sales Belief – Profiles – Personalities 47
12. Attitude Maintained 51
13. Sales 55
14. Putting it Down 59

Summary 63
Tony Russell 65
Valued Sales Training 67

Acknowledgements

I would like to thank all of my colleges who have helped me along the way and also my family for their support and anticipation. The companies I have worked for have more often than not given me a wealth of opportunity to gather the skill set I now obtain and can now share.

N. Messer	J. Brelel	R. Sinton
R. Singla	V. Patel	B. Williams
C. Barron	D. Howard	S. Navaro
J. Hicks	C. Jenkns	A. Puris
P. Balbers	A. Accorda	S. Pasens
T. Belaus	J. Peters	Xlibris Publishig
M. Nikau	E. Porterhouse	

Preface

I wrote this book as a glimpse into the sales world. I think the book has some really great parts to it that show a real glimpse into the inner workings of the sales psyche and that is often hard to do, but in some places I think it has been portrayed quite well within this book. That can be useful in sales to see like minded occurrences and although in most training in sales you often try to shelter pupils from seeing the whole side of the story until they are ready or see for themselves, in this case I thought more on the fast track. Hope the readers enjoy. T. Russell

1

Knowing Sales – We All Know the Story Somehow?

 I'm saying everyone knows what they're doing when they step into sales. Selling ice to eskymos draws a high feeling with most youthful and exuberant monkey men and women! Like a bull at the gate you're ready to get out there and sell your product with eigther tact, precision or persuasion.
 Sales isn't something everyone knows straight away though, even if you have a pretty good idea what you want to do as soon as it crosses your mind taking a position on, understanding it all together is a bit more complicated, and you will work all that out along the way. When I was at school as far back as primary School we use to have a game like charades "If aliens came to earth how would you go about explaining things to them" We don't speak the same language and would not have a whole lot in common so how do you teach them what a kitchen sink is. This is the case a lot of the time in sales, explaining something clearly to someone who knows nothing about it.

Television is a lot to do with an infatuation with sales, its marketing and everything down to the 30c cone at Mc Donald's has influenced our perspective on sales and how we believe it is. Maybe it's movies that develops your interest in sales, maybe that's what turns you away. Then maybe it's because there is just a tone of jobs out there that say 'sales people needed' and 'no experience necessary' that brings your head out of the wood work. And this is probably a big part of a lot of people's interest!

If anyone watches Big bang theory this is a bit like starting out your sales career, it's something that kicks your sales brain into over drive and you are instantly on the journey of developing in the sales industry. Some people spend nights awake with constant thought after a day out, pondering things until they need to count sheep too fall asleep at night. I know I did, and I enjoyed it.

So why do we all seem to know sales so well and at the same time be so open to learning it and hearing what everyone else thinks, and even anyone else.

It is an individual's journey and most likely the more internal you can keep the journey the more you will work out. The sales environment alone causes people that rarely concentrate in school classes to suddenly snap to attention like it is a do or die circumstance. And it could well be in some peoples situation, there are defiantly winners and losers in sales so you don't want to be categorized as a looser whatever that may mean. So you had better make your story work.

A lot of the time your background can determine this perception you have towards your job and that goes along with your immediate influence, your mentors or protojay.

I always had an interest in business and was lucky enough to do up pushbikes instead of just a lemon aid stand for a young experience in business and sales. And noticeably, not that this veered my attention away from the lemonade stand, but it does seem a little more like an advantage.

But my point is somehow amongst the action and perception we all know the story of sales, it is installed within us like a natural element or mind set and the ball is already rolling as you step into the job.

I blame television. I watch shows like White collar and throw it back to sales and the same industry I am in, even still to this day. And back in our day one of the biggest influences into sales markets was loudly the cost of a new pack of sports cards ending with 99 cents or even more so a dozen eggs. It was a huge controversy and some people really hated it, and felt like they were being fooled and made to look silly. Back then there was quite an up roar.

That makes my job really hard because I know it works on me and I have often heard of, and know quite surely for myself that people are likened with being 'emotional buyers'. People don't buy if they are upset and that defiantly becomes a learning curb within sales that is as long as a piece of string.

Having a starting advantage on your sale is as simple as seeing the difference between someone who was offended by being charged 1.99c and someone who said it works. Neither of them right or wrong but two differing personalities.

Knowing sales could also stem right back to the chocolate drive at school. Now there is a sales position! Does anyone know what happened to that person who sold 150 boxes of those chocolates? I got well involved with the party! But I did not do that well, and I am now an actual sales representative. I don't really know what that guy or girl is doing now? I was always thinking what the heck they did to sell 150 boxes of chocolates myself. I think they were always rich people so we said they bought them themselves. But you could nearly bet your fortune that person is somewhere down the tree on a sales market closing for a company.

The importance of having a backing of people that will purchase from you is not something every sales representative has to start with, and nor is it a concern a lot of the time with the ever changing experiences and different jobs most people go through before settling in one position. The origins are a bit like your credit file with the banks and some people are off to a good start right from the word go. I really started my sales experience in Realestate and after a turmoil of ups and downs within my life!

I had nothing in the way of client bases or a great credit reputation so taking the recommendation with the farming of an area is a very important factor to real estate sales.

It doesn't relate to selling to an entire city, it relates to becoming known within the market. A lot of the time your story is going to be similar to the guy next to you like you were all sitting down and watching the wolf of wall st studying it together some people swearing that you don't really want to be like mike all at the same time.

Your story will develop and you will develop your story. And eventually for the successful ones who follow through with their sales theories that you knew right from the start, you'll get somewhere. And then go on to learn and develop yourself to suit the industry successfully. You will not only have written it for yourself you would have also developed the style for your clients and even the new entrants to the market that watch listen or even read from what you are doing. So the wheel begins to turn, and now along with your part in play.

So your starting out and know your sales, and maybe if you look at it from a position of time spent searching for work and racking your brains on the job market like we all do before we even get a job. A positive thought is that the time spent thinking about the job before you get it could be placed down as work experience just for the thought you put into it, and maybe even the reason it takes you so long and so many attempts to get that job in the first place when they clearly liked you from the start, but a small something was just missing! Now knowing what you already know you just need to keep asking yourself WHY, and simply keep thinking about it.

2

Prenumtive Attitude

We talk a lot about attitude in sales and it is an important thing involved in every area of your sales position. Your attitude is going to change throughout the time that you are in your job, and in your right mind even your attitude should really be progressing to adapt to your style of sales your client and the environment.

Attitude is defined as; A predisposition or a tendency to respond positively or negatively towards a certain idea, object, person, or situation.
Attitude influences an individual's responses to challenges, incentives, and rewards.
(taken from - Businessdictionary.com)

You're going to need to develop in both definitions and the main reason behind this is that people are "emotional buyer's". This means that your attitude will affect their attitude and in turn affect sales.

I am looking a little further into the initial starting attitude or 'prenumtive attitude' that goes along with sales and often starts from you initial perception. The best attitude you can develop during your first experience is most defiantly a passive attitude. Sales is considered a cut throat industry, this doesn't mean the client will get there throat cut but more so means that the level of competition between your colleges is very high.

This is like a curve ball you will a lot of the time have to adjust too in order for you to maintain the attitude you have in your initial appointing toward your work. Optimism is one of the key attributes to maintaining a positive attitude toward your job weather that be optimism toward your goals and money or just toward your approach and technique.

The initial form of attitude widely accepted within the sales industry is encouragement, it is a learning environment and people are there to help everyone pursue their goals. Often the encouragement is of achieving big money, but some people "myself one of them" also encourage personal growth.

Money is however a key driver in sales and gives us both incentive and enthusiasm to reach our goals. Money is also going to pull your strings, test you and expose your attitude. You should probably choose wisely how you configure this perspective and you will still need to maintain a positive attitude weather that be in your ability to make money or your approach toward its agenda. I start with thinking why you need money and how hard it would be without it. And from there you can gauge how it affects you your position and those around you, like your customers. A bad attitude or negativity is never going to get you were you want to go hear.

In most cases you're going to be pretty full to the brim with enthusiasm as you step into sales and have a fantastic work Attitude ready to be the star pupil and star representative at the same time. Starting out in this industry is not something that regularly warrants a bad attitude. Anyone with a bad attitude toward this work usually is not here to start with, but as the competition creeps in it will also affect your ethics and in turn of course your attitude. You might not completely know the thoughts behind your colleagues and even teachers, so a lot is left blindly for your perception and your initial sales thoughts and tactics.

So when you start out in sales your pre-emptive attitude toward your position will often be quite solitude. That can change as you notice similarities of other people in the same situation but your technique might and can often set you apart.

There are so many different personalities and techniques for sales that narrowing yourself into your preferred personal approach can be a bit confusing, as specially if you want to achieve the results like the person next to you. There are techniques that some people find easier to approach than others, and in the long run none of them are really right or wrong. Like learning anything you are going to make mistakes along the way and you should probably realise this but not dis regard it.

Attitude maintained is another key concept we use in sales, don't get brought down by others around you or your own poor results as this will only keep you from performing to your best. Remember the differing personalities amongst the team and take your place.

If your able to grease yourself up and get down and dirty selling ice to eskimos straight away with your position that is going to be all well and good, but there is one thing you need to be able to do and that is to smile and maintain a positive attitude while doing it.

Sometimes that is all it takes to make the difference between a successful sales representative and a not so successful sales representative. A lot of maintaining your attitude and even your sales technique can just relate to not having a bad time at work, because no one wants to hate there job. Or even giving a simple smile so someone else does not hate your job.

I have used smiling as a technique to keep trainees on a direct path starting out in sales firstly because it works, but also because the leader is strongly defined buy their results and just ensuring your recruits are smiling at the clients you are sending them too can mean the difference between a few complaint calls or lost sales due to upset customers.

Positivity is the attitude you need for success hear; I'm sure what your doing has crossed your mind already and I'm also sure there was a lot of positive, prepared, willing and able, excited and lucrative concepts about what your about to lead off into. And if you're up and enthusiastic you must be on to something! There must be some merit to it, you just need to maintain it and keep going!

3

Rocks in the Road

Things are going to get tough, have you ever driven a car on an obstacle course or taken a defensive driving course? You're most likely about too! But I wouldn't feel too bad there is not many jobs out there without obstacles. And not many without similar obstacles to sales. This means that every rose has it thorns and you are going to make mistakes. This is also something you will probably have to realize to maintain that attitude that will shine upon your customers.

Surrounding theories will also feed your beliefs in sales, and how it all works and will continuingly influence your learning along the way. I will mention sales belief a lot within this book as I think it is a critical part of knowing yourself as a representative and sorting out things such as the diversity of sales you are targeting, or the industry and even your reflection on your clients. If you want to make it you will have to have someone supporting your methods in most cases.

If your branching out find someone to second your theory, and if you can't your probably wrong. And this is why until you are able to identify the correct sales methods for your product line, you should always stick to the way you are told by your sales trainer even if it doesn't make a lot of sense in some cases.

A lot of people find this hard but if you are ever at a rock in the road that is going to slow you down, doing precisely what you are told by your manager will be a solid identifiable way around nearly any problem. If ever I'm stuck even to this day, I still go back to exactly what I am told and the basics I started from. Leaders have learnt to deal with the *scrutiny* surrounding sales and they have learnt to find ways to protect themselves from it. And as you can imagine they will want to keep you doing the same to realize their margins, so a handed down sales tactic is as good as gold. And after all if you do only what you're told to do and still fail out there, really your landing yourself off the hook.

Here are a few problems you might run into:

Rules: are rampart within sales and not all the time openly noticeable so this can often be one of the first rocks in the road you will find most difficult to either move with or adjust to - no matter your sales methods.

You will have to learn to view things from all angles and adjust yourself to a basic curriculum as well as keep an eye on your performance and how to achieve the best results you can. You already know how you're going to do that though right, because you thought of that before you had started!

Well something is going to change that method you thought was going to work for you, and you will have to adjust some things to getting it done how they are done properly in this environment. Surly you wouldn't be too far from being on the right path to sales greatness if you are in your right mind in the first place! Keeping an eye out on how it has been done before is going to be a direct insight into the way things are run.

Sales trainers: have strong sales beliefs and are often already well set in there ways, and this can be frustrating. A lot of representatives who train sales people really prefer to start with a blank canvass and mould there representatives through their own methods due to their personal sales techniques and even *BELIFE*. This is common because often the team production is best when it is in tune with the operator! This can be an obstacle to some and was often an obstacle to myself being new and not understanding although you do need to get into the groove. Really this industry was built on doing exactly what you are told, sometimes no matter what you are told.

Moral: plays a big part in sales and selling a product or specifically pedalling a product! And can often form a rock in the road. Identifying how to look after your moral is not really as easy as you would think. It is also not really an overnight process and you are bound to make a lot of mistakes no matter how good you are, or how good your sale is. Laying all your cards out on the table is often a well recognized technique. The other is sticking to scripts and doing precisely what you are told like I have mentioned. If you carry your moral in every presentation of yourself to a bitter point, your moral values can become an automatic and critical part of every sale and your sales technique.

The company: Is this were you want to be and do you believe in the company's profile. Firms are sometimes very different in their internal preferences for operation, and even their external preferences for operation. Most companies have a description of their company values and information about the company's background on their website. Read this carefully to work out what the company actually stands for. If you don't agree with what you see from there, it might not be worth your proceeding any further. If you're not in a position to be too choosy about your working preferences I'm sure you will find a way to adjust to the circumstances.

The Product: you will consistently hear that story about that sales representative that did record numbers selling because he truly believed in what he was selling. If you don't believe in what you are selling you should probably first ask yourself *WHY*? It could be something you're not understanding and might warrant some product analysis and engagement to learn more about its advantages and market position. If you still are not interested in the product then reconsider why your there in the first place. You're a critical part of the sales product chain don't be there if you have a weak link and cannot sell. Eigther the product is not for you or it's not worth selling.

Colleagues: the sales structure is also very competitive, your colleagues are really not there to act as a business partner, they are there to be the best. There are many different sales personalities and techniques along with them. Blending in is typical and can lose you in the crowd if your trying to make a name for yourself. But blending in, in a lot of cases is also a requirement. Rocking the boat can land even the best achiever in hot water and in some situations have you out of a job, so make sure you form a strong straight position within the team and slowly work your way to the top if that's where you want to be or even just take your position within the job.

There are hundreds of things you are going to encounter that make it harder to achieve your best result. Sales is a learning process so you can make a bit of room for error for yourself. And there already is quite a bit of room made for error in most cases.

You should probably even use that room for error to your best advantage. But the most important thing you can do is to continue working your way through these *"Rocks in the road"* or problems you occur and there on continue to GROW within the industry. One of the most important factors of the Entry level market is that you are constantly moving forward, if you get left behind your own personal market crashes.

4

Pitch Tones Punctuation and Grammar

This is one of the exciting parts of selling and specifically brings forward the critical embodiment of the selling technique and etiquette, if you're notable enough to notice. Pitch, tone, punctuation and grammar are critical throughout the sales approach. Lead generation such as telesales and solar lead generation have specific script writers that forgo a wealth of industry experience and an eye for precision, placing together a pitch that any one will be able to sell with and do it well, and properly without having even a day's experience. Were sales representatives develop a natural ability to sell properly introducing the product and the company, nearly without even thinking about it. The best way for you to catch on quickly is to follow the plot.

Pitch: There is Pitch then there is the pitch! Pitch is defined as "the quality of a sound governed by the rate of vibrations producing it; the degree of highness or lowness of a tone." Or "the steepness of a slope, especially of a roof."

The pitch is a sales aid! A lot of work can go into structuring a good pitch as a sales aid, as I have mentioned until this day if I am struggling I still go back to the safety of a sales pitch "word for word" The other term described is much the same as using tone, but probably more of a direct and up toned style of what I refer to as really *"talking to the customer"*.

You have to learn how to deliver any pitch or product. Tones, punctuation and grammar need to be right and spoken clearly to the customer. There are a lot of different styles of presentation of the product but your personality will also reflect in your work.

Commonly recognised personality traits:

- Amiable: Friendly, Sociable, Good natured, Agreeable, Kind, Likeable and good-humoured.
- Driver: Teamster, Trainer, Directive, Handler, Assertive, conservative and technical.
- Expressive: Liberal, motivational, flamboyant, sensitive, Dramatic and meaningful.
- Analytical: Technical, Systematic, Conservative, solitary, rational and work orientated.

Your personality traits can sometimes assist you to determine your preferred style, and your characteristics will deliver the pitch *"or Product"* the best way possible to the customer *"Your way"*. Practice in the mirror, it is one of the best ways to watch your expression at the same time, you don't want to scare the customer off with a strange expression. (Check it out)

Using your *TONE* will be about the second thing you should try to grasp. Specifically in the first three seconds of meeting your customer this fits a dramatic effect. The first three seconds with a good tone and manner can turn a disgruntled client into a happy and open customer in only the first three seconds. That's meaning you can also lose your customer in the same time.

Tone should also speak to the customer; If you have made it past the first three seconds make sure your using your *tonality* to speak to the customer, keep them in high spirits. And keep them knowing your own, and their own situation. The better you are with people the easier you will find maintaining a healthy conversation with your customer, but time practice and gruelling repetition will get you there if you are struggling.

The mirror is perfect to take a look at your style, and seeing your own reactions can help you learn to control them. Some people find putting it all together easier than others but your tone should be used to *SPEAK* to your customer clearly and deliver a pitch perfect presentation.

Punctuation on the other hand, apart from the indications from your text. *Punctuation* can probably also best describe knowing when to shut up and when not too. You need to control the conversation as much as you can so placing a full stop silence in your pitch were there should be a comer can leave you un heard. You need to get your sale across but at the same time you don't want to come off rude or too over powering for the customer, again this could cost you the sale.

In a direct form of sales, getting the full presentation across to the customer is in most of the time very necessary. Unless your client was already thinking of buying the product you are going to need to put a bit of sales spin to your presentation, and the best sales spin is to have your product heard. I am not saying to talk over the customer I'm saying to have them gasping to hear more, or so impressed with your presentation and timing they couldn't walk away from you for trying.

And you cannot present to a client without good *grammar*, as much as you want to lean on the post and have a good friendly relaxed sale with your client, the majority of the time people will prefer a professional presentation. You do need to build rapport but make sure some of that rapport is a piece of your professional approach towards your product.

Speak clearly and don't use too much slang, while it is comfortable, it doesn't pay off in the majority of circumstances and one thing in sales that will always broaden your margins is thinking for the majority. Your *grammar* brings clarity to the sales pitch, and speaking clearly and fluently with your customer so they fully understand your product or sale is an absolute necessary part of the sale. The clearer you can describe what you are selling to the customer so they can understand why *YOU* think this is such a great product, the better chance you have of a sale.

5

Developing Technique – Learning Curbs

Just as you get rocks in the road, your going to have to deal with them hear. That is a *learning curve* and every time you make a mistake you should be automatically remembering what happened and thinking of ways to fix it.

I would walk away from a sale were a customer has rejected my proposal for any reason going over what just happened over and over repeatedly with a fine tooth comb in my head. I would meticulously go over each sale in my mind, over and over to know what happened and then again to think of ways I can correct it. Nothing is really text book at this point of viewing your technique and looking back on yourself. So it can sometimes be hard to define, but you will always recognize certain practices and methods used in your sales training that are closely related also methods used by other sales representative, and this will help you to not make the same mistake at the next sale.

Bringing together all of the different techniques you learn from sales training and along with your own personal school of hard knocks isn't easy! It is going to take a lot of time to perfect any technique because you need it so fluent to have it right, it becomes automatic. So you should always relentlessly be trying to improve your skills and better yourself, so you are growing in the industry! For a lot of people starting out in sales, personal development is a strong point of their direction. It is also very central to the way the industry runs, and this doesn't ever change.

You just need to keep up, so continuous learning is as important as making the sales.

One of the easiest described and often most over looked examples of a learning curve you will have to learn is not using slang with your customers and really developing that master piece of your professional approach towards your product. This is often concerns you so not to look robotic or even to not look like a sales representative at all. Trying to be too cool with the customer and trying not to be a sales representative is a very common mistake, and also very costly to yourself and especially when it comes to being part of the sales channel as a whole.

Pretending not to be a sales representative is like carrying a concealed weapon and it makes it harder for a comfortable rapport with your client. So it's never going to work.

Attitude is discussed all the time in sales and represents many different attributes in its *ambiguities*. The main one is merely having a good Attitude at all times just so it rubs off on your colleagues and customers automatically. And that makes a lot of sense because no one wants to be upset during a purchase or their day at work. Your Attitude is also one of your best sales techniques and will make you a lot of fun and friendly sales.

Learning curbs are going to happen, one of the key things is to stay focused and just let it happen and not get upset. Goals will help you to stay focused on to your targets and keep you on track, to keep your learning as focused as you are.

Not wanting to have a bad day at work forced me to develop my technique in my attitude. I would swiftly learn to avoid trouble with the client and there are ways to keep your customer in high spirits so even if they are not interested in what you are doing it still won't drag your day down.

We hear time and time again about how mistakes have to be made time and time over before someone achieves greatness. And it is the same hear. One of the main reasons all these things you are learning just don't come to you straight away and that is that you need to develop your technique to an 'automated function'. You are selling in a relationship with your client and that will become automatic but that will also take time and experience. Like any job you will get better at it the more you continue to do it. Building yourself a sales mind is a defiant process and the more you can positively feed your mind the more you will develop. It doesn't matter if you don't think something is having an affect straight away, you will get there.

Do some research into *sales personalities*; different techniques suit different representatives and there are many different charts and diagrams available online for you to get a good idea of what suites you best. There must be well over a thousand different paraphrases that relate to sales development. Also thousands of rules and guidelines such as the eight steps to success in sales. Diagrams like Maslow's hierarchy of needs and one of my personal favourites the Johari window, which outlines your known self, conscious self, unknown self and unconscious self. And one of the reasons why I think you can just learn without thinking you are learning.

Here are a few tips:

- Practice in front of the mirror
- Ask a friend to help: *Doing sales battels helps develop technique, take a look at your own style and even while acting the customer you can note yourself in that situation.*
- Learn your scripts
- Analyse everything
- Read, watch videos and take note's
- Learn your Product knowledge *A lot of the time this can be pretty limited for you to access, and that is often to protect you the representative from miss understanding. I love more product knowledge and think everyone should gain more product knowledge to represent what's there to their client so much better, but really you must know your immediate equipment very well.*

Continuous learning is undoubtedly the best technique for learning how to be the best sales representative there has ever been. But don't be afraid to branch out from the pack and work for yourself. While a sales team is good, one representative can make a lot of a difference so don't let yourself get too caught up in the team.

Continue working on yourself developing your technique. This can take a long time but anyone can get there even the least achieving students with terrible grade marks often do well in sales.

Remember persistence and attitude can take you a long way.

6

Rapport

I'm going to look a little further into developing your technique with *Rapport*, I call it *Rapport interruption* because often building rapport is something that can really be a challenge and an obstacle to becoming a good sales representative.

I think to start with the easiest or quickest fix for problems with building *rapport* with your client is to try to not think about it while you are doing it. It will just happen and for Door to door sales for example there are small techniques like *ice breakers* that set the tone and a high spirit for your sales pitch - just to get things going. If you want to go one step better you can call *ice breakers* catchphrases instead, this leaves simple ice breakers available to be used at any time.

Rapport is great but in my professional opinion you don't really need to build a lot of *rapport* in sales at all. This is because eigther way when you are doing a presentation it should be on track, strong and professional. That goes for whatever sales method you angel and then from that the *rapport* comes from your knowledge, presentation and proposal! Even the most exuberant and flared sales representative are taking themselves and their delivery very seriously in practice and presentation.

My simple point though is that amongst all of this mention of rapport techniques, people really do not want to build a great deal of *rapport* with you in the first place. If they want or need a product they want or need it simple as that! All they really want to feel is comfortable, and like they are making a good decision. When I have trained people I have often told them to cut *rapport* all together out of their sales tactics and told them to cut straight to the chase to get them to focus more on their work. Otherwise we often find ourselves back like in chapter five holding a concealed weapon, and it doesn't sell products.

So if rapport is not what you are trying to build with your client then what is it? - Well its confidence, and when your talking about rapport building, the confidence to build with your clients is a lot going to be in you as the representative. A couple of things people might be looking for are emotional equalities like your status outside of your job, and common personalities such as family values. A lot of these things are personalised and you won't be able to build on them. If you don't have any common experience in these types of centralised things they can be hard to learn, so many representatives even develop a preference to the personality of their customer.

Experience with different personalities will help you in the long run, but before you get that well involved with your job there are a few simple things you can do to broaden your market. And just doing your job is one of them.

Robotic style sales is a simple way to broaden your sales margins - stick to what you know and what you know works!

Some representatives I have sat down with say nearly the same thing time after time with every sale. In *forty five* mins exactly you would walk away from your client with or without the sale, on time every time, or not at all. And it was done because it worked so it was more likely a sale than walking away empty handed.

So if you don't need a great *'rapport'* with a customer to sell a product, they in a lot of cases don't even need to like you. As long as you tell them about the product clearly, deliver it with purpose and a structured or professional approach you will make the sale. Don't let trying to be too friendly hold you back from doing your job, but at the same time don't represent the team too much as a sales representative. I just try and concentrate on my work.

When I say want or need I also mean keeping the clients moral at a height. They might need to donate to charity once in a while so make sure you include that emotional effect in your list of wants and needs.

7

Attitude

Attitude is a key attribute to have in sales; it is something that links personality with a passion and will influence the sale driving yourself and the client to develop a relationship during a pitch. Attitude has a lot of other purpose within the selling environment also but it is best to keep it simple for the time being.

Simply speaking you *attitude* will rub off on whoever is around you, all of the time - and every time you meet a person. So you need to keep your *attitude* in a good place all of the time and every time you face a client. Then you also need to be thinking positive, and keep the wheels turning that way! As just like negativity breads negativity, a positive attitude is vice versa. Having a bad *attitude* will not only ruin your day it will reflect on the company and the product you are selling. One thing good for keeping a high spirit is to take a look at your target market, and remind yourself all you are going to need is one sale from how many people you think of. Then you can move on to the next one after you have achieved the first concentrating on one at a time "as a simple trick to prevent the *optimistic blues*". I will probably mention time and time again and you have probably heard that people are emotional buyers - your *attitude* is key to that emotional response.

Let's take a look at some different circumstances:

1. Smile through your pitch

e.g. Your speaking to a client face to face at the door of their home or office, you have had a bad day and have not archived any were close to Bills your colleges targets. You have also spoken to over four qualified clients and have not made a successful sale yet. Your getting a bit winey and this reflects to your client straight away as soon as a conflicting line is dealt in your pitch. There's no way the client is going to appreciate your negativity and bad attitude to their objections and formal questions and even if they are very interested in the product they just put it off and ask for a business card from you to try again next time.

Hint: As specially in commercial and business circumstances the customer is often very experienced in working with representatives. Even if you are at a residential premises speaking to a factory hand they have probably spoken to countless different sales people eigther over the phone or at their home. And from that they have caught a jist on how the sales environment functions and how you function. I have always warned my entry level recruits to them being found the armature in the field.

2. Be enthusiastic

e.g. You have a new deal to sell from your company it is a holiday at a fabulous resort at a terrific price and with some excellent rewards to go with it. You are ecstatic to be selling it and this rubs off on your clients over the phone with your enthusiasm and you make record sales that day.

How many times have you heard of that representative who made a lot of money and did really well selling that product, and your only told that he just really believed in the product. His attitude towards what he was selling made countless sales because his enthusiasm and vigour rubbed of with every contact.

3. Be a delight!

e.g. You are in the sales class room, and just like the squeaky wheel gets the grease the happy student often gets the odd secrete or tip. Or just having a good attitude around the work environment makes your collages more willing and happy to help you out.
Along with that, every day you will have a better day at work and the environment keeps you happy so those hard days with no sales are also a lot easier to handle.

These are just the simple measures of your attitude, it gets a lot more complicated than just smiling all day and loving your product. But your attitude is un deniably important.

Another simple example away from just merely being a great person, and a little more focused on your game is an example of your attitude when you are upset with the close of a sale after going through all the work with the client thinking they are going to buy. There is no harm in being a little bit upset if they mention changing their mind so far into the finalization of the sale. So politely mention that you have gone to all this work, and then remind them why they are buying the product in the first place.

Sales can be a hard job and it is easy to get a bit of a bad attitude going, especially running too and forth chasing sales leads. But it is so imperative I couldn't begin to express how important it is to keep your spirits high and maintain a good attitude. To remain focused all the time and to not let the negativity that runs rampart within the industry sway you. I'm not saying not to strive when you need to strive but I am saying everyone else has been there so don't feel too hardly done buy when your given a tough gig.

I will cover a bit more on attitude later in the book as it gets a bit more technical but for now hears a couple of attitude quotes:

"Your attitude is like a flat tyre, if you don't change it you won't go anywhere"
If you are told you have a bad attitude you probably do, so have a look at what your being told and what you need to do to change it.

"Your Attitude is like a price tag, it shows how valuable you are"
This is gold for sure but be careful. It takes experience to have a great effective attitude, if you are going to have an attitude you had better be right to bare that attitude or you will come off arrogant and pushy without a sale.

8

Getting Picky

Really getting to the bottom of what you are doing out there is pretty important. It takes a long time to really develop in the sales industry and things are always changing. One thing that doesn't change is that you will need to deliver a professional sales delivery, build rapport with your client and know what you are talking about.

Getting picky and fine tuning your methods is really a school of hard knocks and is virtually impossible to learn without actual experience with different clients and different circumstances. The biggest thing is that if your not learning from identifying your mistakes then you are not getting anywhere, and that is a problem.

During a sales pitch there are hundreds of things that can go wrong and there are not really enough immediate skills in your training you can use to challenge each circumstance because it is all so vast. One thing is for sure every time you encounter a new problem and deal with that problem it becomes easier the next time you have to deal with it, and you become better at it.

Getting picky with your sales tactics can seem daunting and it is a little daunting at times so try and keep yourself in a positive frame of mind at all times and do not be swayed by outside influences that can make the process harder. Mealy cruse along with the curriculum provided because that is what it is there for and it is great to identify key techniques and jump your memory. The curriculum is a sales aid developed and designed for open training to a whole class of people to help the whole class better identify and utilize their sales skills.

Hears a few tips that will help you really get to the bottom of your sales methods and nut them out so you can fast tune yourself a bit easier:

- **Take notice**
  You should be able to see during any pitch what went wrong! About the best way to overcome any trouble that you encounter is to try your best not to let it happen twice. Leave the sale thinking about what has happened and also contemplating what you will do next time.

- **Take notes**
  You can even write this down so you can look something up online later.

- **Relate them to your curriculum**
  Most of the time there is some part of your training that will have an answer to your problem such as Feel, felt, found, using the jones theory or any of your Gifts and even parts of the eight steps such as maintaining your attitude.

- **Know your curriculum**
  Learn the sales educational curriculum, knowing this off by hand is a great way to fast track your learning. It will make you stand out with your peers and open up new avenues for your work as well as being a fast reminder in the selling situations when you need it.

- **Know your sales type**
  Knowing the style of representative you are and studying different sales personalities will help you get a better idea of how you might be able to do things a little differently next time. And understanding others profiles is good for adding a little spin from a style you are not use to performing. There are literally hundreds on line so try a google search.

- **Watch you tube clips**
  You tube clips are excellent for picking things up and seeing how sales are done properly - type <u>Sales Training</u> into your you tube search take a look, and even get a little inspired.

Another great way to gain new idea and experience is to go out with one of your fellow representatives, most of the time people will be happy to lend a hand and show you what they are doing to become so successful with their work.

Just observe the sale and try it for yourself next time you are selling to a client. Asking questions has always been a stand out quality of a successful representative weather that be of the product or sales techniques.

There is no point beating yourself up over something that trips a sale if you can determine what went wrong. If you can see what happened during the sales *"and customers speak quite clearly a lot of the time"* you will know where you went wrong, and that is one of the biggest leaps in your learning you can make day in and day out.

9

The Grove

The *grove* is brilliant, the grove is getting on a fast paced wave and riding it fluently all the way to shore without even having to think about it. It can take a really long time to develop that perfect *grove* and you will have this happen many times along the way just learning before you really nail it. And that right before things change and you find more you need to work on.

Getting yourself into a grove is something I haven't really heard discussed a lot in sales books, posts and discussions. I call it a grove because it is often repetitive and considered boring even sometimes un mastered and as specially to new enthusiastic sales representatives. Mainly because a script is just a script, but you will defiantly get in the grove all the same. Being in a good and positive state of mind for your work is a really great thing! It mixes in with your positive attitude and becomes critical to your productivity.

When I think of this state of mind or function that I get myself going in, I think of times when I have dis concerned myself with my work, being happy just doing my job and most importantly just knowing that I'm doing it well because I know what I'm doing. Nothing phases me when I have my grove on, and I am just happy to fly along doing my job and I know it's going to work, and also - that I have absolutely nothing to worry about like reaching my targets.

Repetition is a major player getting yourself into a good grove and some of the reason why we give scripts to the newbies in entry level. I like to think we do this because we have you doing things so right you can't possibly do it any better so the way it's being presented cannot be improved upon at all. And really that closely happens *a lot* in the delivery of a product "Believe it or not"! That has to make you feel pretty good about what your doing, and pretty confident in what you are doing too. Also if it really is that good! You are going to meet your sales targets aren't you. To deliver a statement clearly and to its best sense, I often use repetitive sentences to explain things.

So what makes up a good grove and how do you achieve it:

Most of the time a good *grove* is going to be made up by sticking at the one job for a long enough time "to be really good at it". But no matter what, one thing that you have to have to get yourself flying this straight in an un stoppable *grove* is to know your stuff and know your pitches.

The **curriculum** designed for sales is very broad and can sometimes work from a firm level way beyond our end of the job. Recognising the use of scripts and pitches straight through your curriculum definitely provides a foundation for you to quickly grasp the concept behind sales. The curriculum is something that is going to give you a quick trail tuition to sales tactics and procedures. Of course learning it is more or less essential to developing in the industry, but it is not the only part you are going to have to master. Remember you really need to work on yourself as a strong rule.

You are going to have to **know your product** pretty well, and your **industry** is going to be a good thing to grasp so you have a good idea how things work, then from studying pitches and curriculum to improve your own sales lines you will start to develop a functional *grove*.

But things consistently change in sales and that's the same in most industries. So that means a good *grove* can be interrupted pretty easily by several different factors surrounding your work, like a change of regulation by the government or a new team leader. And a complete change of your product that you use means your going to have to study up quickly. There are also thousands of things that will distract you in the everyday environment.

Once in tune with all of this along with UNDERSTANDING your industry, from there on in you will be able to perform wonders no matter the weather or abrupt change!

After practice you can nail the ice breaker right on time and use the best of punctuality, and also tone with each customer. And above all know what you are talking about to handle any objections. Knowing more about your product is always going to be the best way to land any advice that is going to be key to gaining a sale.

Even if sometimes you wish you did not know something to make it easier, there really is a reason for every product on the market and for the flow of your grove you are also going to need to understand this.

It's a great feeling, it's a relaxing feeling and it's something that you will be happy to achieve but it will take time and effort, also a little time and knowing what you are doing to perform to your best.

10

Your Technique – With Industry Knowledge

After you have been in sales for an amount of time you will start to develop a knowledge of the industry you are in and the general sales industry itself. Now developing this into your *technique* should be getting down to a fine art. The thing with industry and sales knowledge is that it really has been around for a long time, there are millions of technique's and methods and styles, even rules. These are of course different for each specific industry you're in and even differ between the area you work within for your employer, the demographic that you cater too is also a factor to consider.

I have done the exact same position for the exact same job in a different company and found myself targeting a completely different market selling the same thing, and so of course I had to use a different sales style all together just due to the expectations of the clients when they are approaching you or being approached.

The technique you use should be adaptable to the different demographic you are marketing too. I have mentioned before markets being differentiated a lot buy their online presence these days. People's perception of a company can differ from what search engine they find you on and specifically the style of web page your company has in view too the public's eye.

If your home page has pictures of a home brew kit on the front page that is going to send a certain message to your clients *"as a notable example"* This might not directly affect your sales market, but it does influence it.

Developing and doing time in the industry gives you an ora that is easily noticeable to the client also. Some lucky people have this automatically, or at least seem confident when you are not so sure of yourself. Simply learning and learning as fast as you can, will give you the confidence you need to step up to the level of being a more confident and experienced representative.

When I was in sales, and had spent a long time in the industry I called it *intellectual capital*. Gaining intellectual capital apart from time, will come from any source as long as you are looking for it or being part of it. Like reading news in the paper or email feeds. In most cases a rooky representative won't have all the access they want to the information they really need to stand out from the crowed and excel at their job. These days it is a bit easier, now there are ample websites and different forums posting information about nearly any industry you could ever imagine, but it can still be a struggle.

You have easy access to all of your products and even your competitors that are in the industry. Knowing your competitor's advantage is essential to selling your product and highlighting the reason why your product is designed how it is, and why they should pick you over the competitor will win you sales.

Get amongst it as much as you can, defiantly including the sales industry along with general product training. Hearing how your *Sales Competitors* are handling things will tweak your interest and tweak your performance, everyone is always happy to assist you as much as they can and training is an excellent way to develop yourself in marketing and sales. Most people are often itching to train the next top representative.

There are literally thousands of marketing and sales tips posted across the internet and *you tube*, and there is always some big names in sales and business to spur you to achieve in your industry. And don't forget books!

There is plenty of information available on websites: on one website there are ten listed sales techniques that will work. Specifically discussing your *technique* with industry knowledge at this point I have narrowed it down to three - plus just for a look a very significant replicate of the topic in a statement made directly from the world renowned Steve Jobs - who stated...

"Be a yardstick of quality. Some people aren't used to an environment where excellence is expected" – Steve Jobs

It might not work perfectly but it also shows that the shock of a knowledgeable representative with a mass of industry experience can help, and how that will be noticed. And furthermore some clients will be willing to sign at nearly any price only minutes from meeting you.

Sales Techniques:

7. Starting a client relationship (Sales method)

This shows that once the first contact is made, you will need to build the client relationship. Also saying it is important to listen and to understand the client's business needs, and this being more than easy with a wealth of industry knowledge. Then once you've built that relationship, shown you understand, you can know that you have earned their trust.

9. Remember a promise is a promise (Sales method)

If you promise to do something discussing a sale with a client, maybe a favour relating back to your services/product or even conditions, make sure you follow through. *Bat for your client*
You can stand in court for your client, you word is close to being as strong as the paper you have people sign upon. E.g. - If you say they can sign now and pay later if they choose. This is in cases as good as the document they have in their hand! And this works in a lot of cases, not all - but a lot and your experience should know the difference.
The main point is that "Now" you are part of the industry, you need to become a working mechanism within the industry for whatever the situation may be. You defiantly have a certain amount of power as a performing representative.

10. You are the expert (Sales method)

Don't forget that you're the expert, make sure you exert this in all forms and that the client knows that they can turn to you for advice. This will see you make countless sales as long as you are the industry expert and once again have the knowledge to provide your client with expert advice.

Ok so your technique should change a bit with industry knowledge, this only makes sense if you're getting better at your job as you continue to gain experience. Keep things truthful but use your experience and power with your knowledge! *(To your best advantage.)* Rightfully both you and your client should be happy with the returns.

11

Sales Belief – Profiles – Personalities

I call it a belief, I have a firm belief that when we are talking about sales or performing sales I know what I'm doing or what I'm talking about and above all I know what the industry is about.

It is a belief in what you are doing. Eigther a belief in your product *(as you will have to begin with)*, or as you continue to grow in the industry, a belief in how you are growing within the industry. Just like we grow older as children and believe in *Santa clause*, in sales things tend to change along the way both with your personality and with your position within the industry, such as management positions.

Sometimes it is hard to know what truth is and what isn't when it comes to Sales. A lot of the time it is not as complicated as things sometime come across - and other times it is. If you have ever heard of the poem *'desiderata'* this leads a good example, and a great example to guide your mind through nearly every aspect in life.

The simple foundations are simply the best and most specific way to stay direct and stay on the right track when your dealing with sales styles, sales tactics, and as specially in sales beliefs.

Different profiles and personalities in sales in the long run really are not that differentiating. And as a long term sales representative one of my beliefs is that eventually all professional sales representatives end up very close to similar within the industry, and there really is not a lot that forms a great difference between successful top sales reps.

You are more than likely familiar with the sales method or belief termed _Straight line business sales_ and this is very specific to the way most successful sales representatives operate. If you google it or put the phrase into a YouTube search engine I am sure it will pop up.

I have developed a similar model to guide sales representatives that is close to being of a similar nature but instead of guiding yourself across the field it is developed as a pyramid were we head straight up and recognize the process from the ground level. From there highlighting the path to ending up at the top as a professional, direct and sucessfull sales representative. I am not introducing it in this book but I will explain the model in detail with another publication later down the track.

There are of course a lot of different beliefs and personalities, and no one right answer is going to be correct all the time. There is a difference within segments of the industry than require you to adjust your style accordingly to suit your position.

So I will define the term belief:

Belief as defined by Google search engine is:

> An acceptance that something exists or is true, especially one without proof.
> "His **belief in** extra-terrestrial life"
> - Something one accepts as true or real; a firmly held opinion.
> "We're prepared to fight for our beliefs"
> Or: trust, faith, or confidence in (someone or something).
> "A belief in democratic politics"

I use to know a guy in sales who would preach quit often in a cryptic but direct fashion, and one of the things he use to really believe was that *"if you think it is true than it is"* plain and simple. While he might have been a little bit loose on the cannon it really is pretty accurate to sales as long as you stay on track.

The foundations of sales lie within your own personality, and we often achieve results from people with similar characteristics from us. But in the beginning of your sales experience this will be very consistent. You are the one noting your sales and the tactics you use to achieve the results, so who else to know better than yourself what is happening when you are doing well and achieving your best.

Without proof though you will not go a long way in the sales industry as it is driven highly on results so the sooner you can distinguish the belief that is forming and put it to practice - the better off you are going to be.

That sheds a bit of light on the first term of belief but what about the second:

If you are to have a faith trust or confidence in something in sales that would form a recognisable belief and one of the first you will notice is that *"if you approach 150 customers speak to 70 of that 150 and from that 70 people 30 showed interest and from that 30 you achieved 9 sales."* Just simple numbers! The more people you approach the better your chances are of seeing the results you need.

There has to be more to it than that though and working out what else is a firm belief that you can have trust, faith and confidence in is nearly the whole developmental strategy of sales all together.

The bottom line is you cannot really believe something that isn't really true, even if it is only truthful to yourself, but you can work out what is working best for you and that makes whatever you think working true. Once you work out what you can do to gain results within the industry to achieve what you want from your role within sales. Then performing to that standard is going to be what is generating your sales and results, and generating of course your income.

12

Attitude Maintained

This is the third time I have mentioned attitude in this book so I would say that expresses its importance. Attitude maintained is one of the steps outlined in sales curriculum that more or less tells us that we need to act right, and also have that solid conviction and confidence to consistently achieve high standards. This time we look a bit further beyond just smiling and loving your work but still without maintaining a great day at least for yourself to come home happy you might as well go back to the first time I mentioned Attitude. No matter how hard it is to keep smiling you can't progress until you nail that positive attitude.

This time we have a look at the bit sometimes closely familiar to were you start getting into your grove going. And from that, is where that attitude when you are in that grove also needs to remain clean and consistent.

Maintaining a healthy attitude is being on top of your game, assisting your client were its needed and knowing what you are doing and why you are doing it. The tricky part is keeping a good relationship with your client at the same time, all the time staying focused.

Things like defending your product or company can become a natural instinct, but to develop it properly you need to realise the sensitivities of your client before you realise your own. The customer is always right, as specially with face to face consumer sales were you have not built a great rapport personally with the client and they really don't have much more to go on but their personal research. The market is more than often flooded with competition and standing out from the crowed is in the majority of cases left to you the sales representative.

Your attitude is critical to the sale nearly each and every time, finding a dead fish happens but not nearly enough to live on. It is a little like talking to your client, not just selling them or talking at them with your product line. But really *"talking"* to the client, having them see your position and your roll within the presentation.

While this assists your sale it also relaxes the customer and helps them be confident in a healthy decision. Professionalism might come across too robotic sometimes and people don't really like talking to a robot as specially when spending good amounts of money.

A typical example of a good sales attitude is taking a bit of offence to assumptions like your being there to rip them off. It's not a good way to make sales if you come across cavalier to caring about what you are doing, so you have to figure some way to tackle an encounter that is going to ruin your trust and strip confidence from the customer.

That can more than often be best realized with a bit of attitude, to let them know you are present and accounted for.

That is Attitude discussed three times now from three different ways of looking at the meaning and it's use. It is pretty critical and often very hard to maintain throughout your work. People have bad days and develop problems in life that normally show up in parts of your attitude and even towards your work, and this is more prevalent when it comes to sales because you are dealing directly with people. It's not like having a grumpy day at the car wash, you won't be able to make sales if your yelling at your customer, so a good and correct attitude at work is always, pretty important!

13

Sales

Sales isn't always a the most glamourous of jobs, and sometimes your going to have to get down and dirty. But no matter the sale your doing straight up selling is always going to be the best way to get the job done with the best outcome you can achieve. The market is competitive and one of the biggest problems is that once someone gets the hint on something new in the industry, no matter what it is, it's used like a weapon to destroy the competition. It's like having the Intel in a war that is going to make all the difference, the problem lies in how long it takes you to get with the program so your not caught out and falling behind.

Amongst the clutter there are a few basic truths that can help you go gangbuster on your sales, for yourself and your company:

Number 1.

One of the easiest and even the most helpful things you can do to grow in sales and being a sales representative is actually BEING a sales representative! It still links to attitude if you can see that and as clearly as it represents your style, in the end its one card you nearly always want dealt out on the table.

It's not so bad, take a bit of pride in yourself and your work and it WILL reflect in your achievements. But if ever there was a hard truth in this job - well this is it, because you cannot be in sales without being a salesman.

Number 2.

Another basic truth is that the industry is very competitive, that is the way it is and about the only way your going to not fall behind and not be caught out is to understand the competition within the industry. Winning a sale doesn't come easy without winning the whole game, the industry as a whole always has a staggered effect on its position in the market. Every business usually has its place so you need to find your competitive advantage and bring that on board. This is one of my favourite parts of the Industry, I think we really have a front row seat to business and all of its ups, downs, in's and out's.

That's two easy facts about the industry. Your sales will reflect the industry and customers usually like to have a bit of useful information thrown at them just so they can learn a bit about what is happening. You can use everything to your advantage if you perfect your eye for opportunity.

And this works well in your favour because if you can teach your client something they did not know they will be confident in you as an agent to buy from now and in the future. That is why being straight and strong with your sales works, it is credible and positive like you are a part of the production line they are buying from.

Moving forward in sales and learning is what is really going to get you were you are going. The sales design I prefer to resemble is one that I designed because it really is a slow learning process. You are going to make mistakes along the way and you are just going to have to learn from them. On your way to the top of the scale of your selling you are going to have to continue to learn after making mistakes, often taking a bit of time to veer back onto the right track to shoot too the top of the league of being a sales superstar, but not everybody makes it!

People are going to fall off the line and fail along the way not making the most of themselves and in turn not making the sales they could.

If there is only one way to skin a cat you need to be as close to doing it that way as possible, to make the most of yourself and do the best in your work. It is a hard grasp for a saying to take on board and probably not the easiest way not to plague your mind with problems. But when learning in sales if you are not looking for your mistakes you are never going to learn how to change your habits, so being a little rough on yourself is the best way to keep moving forward.

Sales is selling your product with enthusiasm and selling it with a direction that makes you the professional. There really are a variety of methods to selling and in all reality there are probably a lot of them.

But eigther way your going to need to do it properly, and in the long run I think we all resemble similar traits as sales representatives.

14

Putting it Down

There are always parts within the job that are going to get you moving in a forward and strong motion. You can look at each different sales line as a set, ready to be discovered. So set yourself up to find the best way possible to achieve results.

Managers are often the source for creating the methods to the sales and when you are given product training it is often really overlooked or not quite right to your preferences. Taking a day off to sit down and get amongst the product line and competition to work out your best sales method is a great way to get yourself an advantage over your competition.

Look for tactics and angles you can do during your presentation to increase your chance for a sale. Things like raising the price so you can reduce it to make a bargain sale for the client. Some of the time you will find that this is factored in to your commissions so take a bit of time to do some personal sales statistics to work out what you can achieve for the week *"how many sales"* and what cuts you can make to the price so you will increase your chances for a sale, and at the same time increase the number of sales you can achieve then putting yourself in a better profit margin.

Sometimes there are small things in your product line that are advantageous to your selling, I have used things like the intensions of the company behind the product you use witch can be sometimes easily found on company websites. Foreclosing a company's mission statements "or pieces of them" is a great way to make yourself stand out against your competitor.

If no one knows who is going to tell them? Most people don't really consider this in overlooking product information but it can be presented in a quick one or two words in a matter of seconds during a presentation giving you a key advantage.

Putting it down, really the management is working for you *"or should be"* so check your processes and there should be a *RIGHT* way to sell that particular product. It can take a bit of study to work out the best method and although one way might work a little better for one person, there should be no limit to your development to decipher a way to maximise your technique and in turn maximise your sales.

Consider:

- **Margin cutting:** Give the buyer something so that they feel happy with their purchase, getting a bargain is always a great feeling, nearly as good as getting one over the sales representative.

- **Product differentiation:** Find the key *attributes* that set you apart from the competition.

- **Processes:** Always have a plan! Get yourself into a grove that you are familiar with and know down to a fine art, you will not fumble during a presentation then and will always be on top of your game.

- **Use the school yard principle**: Not everyone believes this but try to keep your life outside of your work as professional as your job while you are at work. So don't smoke in your uniform and if you do - do it well

- **Be committed:** keep a strong commitment to eigther your product or your company, this will keep you in line with being at work and focused on the processes and differentiation. It will also highlight your customer's belief in their purchase from you.

- **Role play:** Some of the best techniques you can get are from mimicking other sellers, you know they work and it makes it that bit easier to get across with something proven.

- **Be involved:** Weather it be your product or just the industry, try to always be doing something that is keeping you within the industry and being an active participant.

- **Research:** Read what you can on anything surrounding your occupation, you will always have something to learn as things are always changing and there is always something you don't already know.

- **Be skill centred:** no matter what remember you are the master of your own talents. Don't hand any power over that you don't need to or you will lose track in what you are supposed to be focused on doing. This is a job and a skill, that it be a sales skills or the mastery of working with people – never switch off.

Sales is a fantastic job, it is also very lucrative. We work closely with people from within and outside of the industry. You meet new and exciting clients all the time make friends and can often really assist your customers in countless ways.

Sales has also been known as a therapy for people suffering things like their confidence with people or confidence with themselves. I have travelled the country and stayed in countless different places on working *"Vacations"* and often done it quite comfortably. With a great reputation towards your work from the management teams, you can be appreciated for the hard work with not only a good wage but also awards, fine dinners and stature.

Get amongst it and sell like you're the top dog in the industry, make money make friends make acquaintances, clients and connections. It's fast paced, enjoy the ride and don't let yourself get tossed out of the car.

And Remember "Always keep your eye on the ball"

Summary

This is a lot to grasp, in all reality there is as much as three year's development along this process within these pages. So don't be too hard on yourself, it takes a long time to develop a fluent and automatic sales driven mind, be confident you will get there and I'm sure you will. Sales is always in search for the incredible.

Tony Russell

Tony has spent many years perfecting his sales styles in his business ventures extending from Business Brokerage, Internet start-ups, telephone and also solar sales. Consistently achieving high standards and high numbers week in and week out selling.

Now Tony has placed just a small part of his expertise into his first sales training book and is expecting more to follow. The content has already helped representatives he has trained and worked with adding up to three hundred percent to their margins. For a short read this sales Manuel is absolutely packed with industry knowledge from Tony Russell a long time proven instructor and selling consultant.

Valued Sales Training

The book is a short journey through the sales process. The ups and the downs you will inevitably encounter from starting out selling in your first position and to light the path to bringing you up to speed toward becoming a professional representative in any field as soon as you can.

The short sales training book is loaded with industry secrets and factual knowledge that will save you countless time spent from learning things the hard way, and will assist to shoot your sales career off to a flying start.

The first of what will soon become a volume of different sales manuals from Tony Russell the best thing you can do is take a look for yourself.

www.ingramcontent.com/pod-product-compliance
Lightning Source LLC
Chambersburg PA
CBHW021016180526
45163CB00005B/1983